The Golden Book of

FLORENCE

MUSEUMS - GALLERIES - CHURCHES
PALACES - MONUMENTS

BONECHI

© Copyright
CASA EDITRICE BONECHI
Via Cairoli 18/b - 50131 Firenze - Italia

E-mail: bonechi@bonechi.it - Internet: www.bonechi.it

English translation:
Erika Pauli *for* Studio Comunicare, Florence.

Printed in Italy by Centro Stampa Editoriale Bonechi.

Photographs from the Archives of Casa Editrice Bonechi taken by:
Gaetano Barone, Carlo Cantini, Paolo Giambone, Stefano Giusti, Italfotogieffe, Antonio Lelli, Andrea Pistolesi, Antonio Quattrone, Alessandro Saragosa, Soprintendenza Archeologica per la Toscana, Soprintendenza ai Monumenti di Firenze.

ISBN 88-7009-426-X

* * *

A view of Florence from Monte alle Croci (Giovanni Signorini, Museo di Firenze com'era.

HISTORY

The river Arno cuts its way through the broad plain on which Florence lies, surrounded by the out-hills of the Tusco-Emilian Apennines. Already occupied in prehistoric times, as early as the 8th century B.C. an Italic peoples with a Villanovan culture settled in the area between the Arno and Mugnone rivers, but little is known of these remote times. In 59 B.C. the Roman city was founded with the square ground plan of the castrum. The decumanus maximuswas laid out along what are now the Via del Corso, the Via degli Speziali and the Via Strozzi, while the ancient cardo corresponds to the line between Piazza San Giovanni, the Via Roma and the Via Calimala. With the arrival of the barbarians, Florence was first besieged by the Ostrogoths (405) of Radagaisus, who plundered the surrounding countryside, although Florence managed to resist and Stilicho's troops inflicted an overwhelming defeat on the enemy. Next came the Byzantines, who occupied Florence in 539, and the Goths who took over the city in 541. Under Lombard domination (570) it managed to safeguard its autonomy, while under the Franks the number of inhabitants diminished and the city lost most of its territory. Around the year thousand, things began to change for the better and the "lily" city's rise continued for various centuries in spite of numerous controversies, wars and internecine struggles. New walls surrounded the city, new civic and religious buildings went up, and at the same time the arts, literature, and trade continued to prosper. In 1183 the city became a free commune, even though it had already actually availed itself of this freedom for many years. The first clashes between the two factions, Guelph and Ghibelline, date to those years. The former were followers of the Pope, the latter of the Emperor. The ensuing struggles were to lacerate the civic fabric of the city up to 1268. Despite the unstable social and political situation, this period witnessed an upsurge in the arts and in literature. This was the time of Dante and the «dolce stil novo», of Giotto and Arnolfo di Cambio. In the 15th century the city's rise continued. Florence was a trading city but also the new cradle for Italian and eventually European culture. Many powerful families (the Pitti, Frescobaldi, Strozzi, Albizi) vied for supremacy in the city. One above all soon came to the fore, a powerful family of bankers - the Medici - and beginning with the founder Cosimo I, later known as the Elder, they were to govern up to the first half of the 18th century, transforming Florence into a beacon during the period of Humanism and the Renaissance. Great personalities such as Leonardo da Vinci and Michelangelo characterized the period and Florentine prestige reached its zenith.
In 1737 the Medicis gave way to the house of Lorraine and the government continued along the lines of a moderate liberalism even if at that point the great period of Florentine culture was on the wane. In 1860, during the Risorgimento, Tuscany was annexed to the Realm of Italy with a plebiscite. For a brief period Florence then became the capital of the new nation.

Facing page and above: Brunelleschi's dome and the Duomo.

THE CATHEDRAL

DUOMO

Dedicated to S. Maria del Fiore, the Cathedral is the fruit of the dedicated work of the many artists who collaborated in its building for various centuries. In 1294 the Corporation of the Guilds commissioned Arnolfo di Cambio with the realization of a new Cathedral that was to replace the extant church of Santa Reparata. The cathedral workshop grew up around and inside the church, which continued to be used for decades, until 1375. Work on the new Cathedral or Duomo began on Sept. 8, 1296 and continued under various *capomastri* or directors of works such as Giotto, Andrea Pisano, Francesco Talenti, until 1375, when Santa Reparata was torn down and part of Arnolfo's project was altered. The **dome** had to wait until 1420, the year in which Brunelleschi won the competition for the building of this enormous structure. In 1434 work was terminated and two years later the church was consecrated, 140 years after it had been begun. The **lantern** was started in 1445 and finished in 1461 with the gilded sphere. The facade is in 19th-century Gothic style.

DOME

Brunelleschi's masterpiece, planned and raised between 1420 and 1434, put the finishing touch on the building of the Duomo. The great artist proposed to build the enormous airy dome without the use of fixed centering, thanks to the employment of ribbing with tie beams and bricks set in herringbone patterns, a double shell for the dome with an ogive form (at the drum the dome is 45.52 m. in diameter and 91 m. high) on a tall drum. The interior of the dome, which Brunelleschi envisioned bare, was frescoed by Vasari and Zuccari (1572-1579). In the 19th century, and recently, proposals have been made to restore the dome to its original pristine whiteness. The **lantern** was also designed by Brunelleschi and is in the form of a temple, raising the total height of the church to 107 meters.

GIOTTO'S CAMPANILE

The Cathedral bell tower was begun in 1334 by Giotto, who as *capomastro* was overseer for the construction of the Duomo.

Up to his death in 1337, he built the bottom part of the campanile comprised of two closed stages decorated with hexagonal and rhomboid *reliefs,* by Andrea Pisano, Luca della Robbia, Alberto Arnoldi and workshop. The relief panels on the lower band, now replaced by casts, represent the *Life of Man* with *Genesis* and *Arts and Industries* executed by Andrea Pisano and Luca della Robbia to Giotto's designs.

The two upper stages were carried to completion by Andrea Pisano, who took Giotto's place at the time. He created a series of sixteen niches between the pilaster strips which contained statues of the *Prophets, Sibyls* and the *Baptist,* surmounted by an equal number of false niches. Between 1350 and 1359 Francesco Talenti finished the campanile, adding two levels with the two gabled two-light windows with their lovely twisted columns and the stage with the single three-light opening.

DUOMO

FACADE

Arnolfo di Cambio's unfinished facade of the Duomo was torn down in 1587. From then on, for almost three centuries, there was a continuous flow of projects and competitions for the new facade of the Cathedral until finally in 1871 the design presented by the architect Emilio de Fabris was approved (work ended in 1887). The facade betrays the historical point of view which ruled the taste of the times and employed the same types of marble previously used in the rest of the building - Carrara white, Prato green and Maremma pink. Above the three portals with *Stories of Mary* are three lunettes with, from left to right, *Charity,* the *Madonna with the Patron Saints of the City,* and *Faith;* the pediment over the central portal has a *Madonna in Glory.* The statues of the *Apostles* and of *Mary* are set in the frieze that runs between the rose windows at the sides and the one in the center. Above, after a series of busts of artists, is the pediment with the low relief of *God the Father.*

Above: the interior of the Duomo of Florence. Below: the bust of Filippo Brunelleschi. Facing page, above: the panel by Domenico di Michelino with Dante and the Divine Comedy; below, left: equestrian monument to Niccolò da Tolentino, fresco by Andrea del Castagno, and, on the right, Paolo Uccello's Monument to John Hawkwood (Giovanni Acuto), fresco.

DUOMO

INTERIOR

In line with the dictates of Italian Gothic architecture there is a strong feeling for vertical and horizontal space inside the Duomo (the fourth largest church in the world: 153 meters long, 38 meters wide across the nave and aisles, and 90 at the transept). In the nave and aisles, piers with pilaster strips support large moderately pointed arches and ribbed Gothic vaulting. A gallery on corbels runs along on high. At the back is the high altar (by Baccio Bandinelli) surrounded by three apses or **tribunes**, each subdivided into five rooms. The polychrome marble pavement (1526-1660) is by Baccio and Giuliano d'Agnolo, Francesco da Sangallo and others. The two equestrian monuments (frescoes transferred from the wall) of John Hawkwood (Giovanni Acuto) and Niccolò da Tolentino are on the wall of the left aisle. The former, of 1436, is by Paolo Uccello; the latter, of 1456, by Andrea del Castagno (note the diversity in the modelling of the figures of these two mercenary captains: severity as opposed to vitality). To be noted among the many other works are the Tomb of Antonio d'Orso by Tino di Camaino (1321); the lunette with the Crowned Madonna by Gaddo Gaddi; and in the left aisle the tabernacle with Joshua by Ciuffagni, Donatello and Nanni di Bartolo; the Bust of Squarcialupi by da Maiano, the panels with Saints Cosmas and Damian by Bicci di Lorenzo.

Above and left: two stretches of the walls of the old Cathedral of S. Reparata in the subterraneans of the Duomo. Facing page, above: the tomb of Filippo Brunelleschi, and, below: fragments of a fresco with the Passion of Christ.

SANTA REPARATA

The old cathedral of Florence was originally built in the 4th-5th centuries on the ruins of a Roman domus, with columns dividing the nave from the two side aisles and a single apse. During the Byzantine wars the church was destroyed, to be rebuilt between the 7th and 9th centuries. The perimeter remained almost the same but the building was enriched by two side chapels and the columns were replaced by piers with engaged pilasters. Between the year 1000 and 1100 a crypt was added under the apse and the choir was raised, while two bell towers were built near the apse. When the new Cathedral of Santa Maria del Fiore was built, this ancient church, dedicated to the young saint who died a martyr in Caesarea, had to relinquish its site. The new Cathedral however was built around the old church which was not torn down until its completion in 1375. In 1966 when the pavement of the Duomo had to be restored, remains of the preceding cathedral came to light. Now an entrance situated between the first and second piers of the right aisle of the Duomo leads down into a spacious chamber where, thanks to the structures installed by the architect Morozzi, the remains of *frescoes* which once decorated the church, the *tombstones* of various prelates and civil authorities (as well as the slab which indicates *Brunelleschi's tomb*), and stretches of the brick and mosaic pavements can still be seen.

BAPTISTERY

This octagonal building with semicircular apses, raised on a stepped podium, was originally built in the 4th-5th centuries near the north gate of Roman Florence. Its current appearance dates to the 11th-13th centuries: the smooth pyramidal roof was terminated in 1128, the **lantern** with columns dates to 1150, the rectangular **tribune** (the « *scarsella* ») to 1202. The exterior is faced with green and white marble. Each side is divided into three sections by pilaster strips surmounted by trabeation and round arches with windows. Particularly striking are the bronze *doors* and, inside, the *mosaics* in the dome. There are three sets of doors in the Baptistery of San Giovanni: the **south doors** by Andrea Pisano with *Stories of the life of the Baptist* and *Allegories of the Virtues,* the **north doors** by Ghiberti, with *Stories from the New Testament, Evangelists* and *Doctors of the Church,* and the **east doors** (or **Gates of Paradise**), Ghiberti's masterpiece and deservedly the most famous of the three. They are divided into ten panels which depict *Stories from the Old Testament* and were commissioned by the Arte dei Mercanti in 1425. In the perfection of execution, they are worthy of the name Michelangelo bestowed on them. Small figures of biblical personages and *portraits of contemporary artists* are to be found in the frame around the panels.

Facing page and on this page: various views of the Baptistery of S. Giovanni.

GATES OF PARADISE: EPISODES FROM THE OLD TESTAMENT DEPICTED IN THE TEN PANELS.

Creation of Adam and Eve. The Fall. The Expulsion from Paradise.	Work of the first men. Sacrifice of Cain and Abel. Cain kills Abel. God reproves Cain.
Noah and his family offering sacrifice after having left the ark. Drunkenness of Noah.	The Angels appear to Abraham. Sacrifice of Isaac.
Birth of Esau and Jacob. Sale of the birthright of the first-born. Isaac orders Esau to go hunting. Esau out hunting. Rebekah counsels Jacob. Isaac is deceived.	Joseph sold to the merchants. Discovery of the cup of gold in Benjamin's sack. Joseph reveals himself to his brothers.
On Mount Sinai Moses receives the Tables of the Law.	The people of Israel in the River Jordan. The Fall of Jericho.
Battle against the Philistines. David kills Goliath.	Solomon receives the Queen of Sheba.

GATES OF PARADISE

The Gates of Paradise are currently being restored and a perfect copy has been set in their place. The photos published were taken of the originals and show the panels in their original splendor before atmospheric agents and pollution covered them with a black patina. The doors there now are bright and shiny and this is probably what they looked like when first placed in the Baptistery in 1425. Eventually they too will be covered by a patina while the restored originals will remain safely sheltered in the Museo dell'Opera del Duomo.

Drunkenness of Noah.

Creation of Adam.

Cain killing Abel.

Sibyl and a biblical personage.   *Isaac orders Esau to go hunting.*   *Discovery of the gold cup.*

BAPTISTERY

INTERIOR

The interior of the Baptistery is characterized by the walls
on two orders, the inferior one with columns and the
upper one with pillars between mullioned windows.
The surfaces are covered by marble geometrical tarsias,
similar to those of the floor. Particularly interesting the
tomb of the Antipope John XXIII, a complex built by
Michelozzo and Donatello (the latter made the reclining
statue), two *Roman sarcofagi* and the tomb *slab of Bishop
Ranieri.* The **apse** is enriched by beautiful *mosaics* of the
thirteenth century, coeval to those of the large dome. Next
to the large *Enthroned Christ* by Coppo di Marcovaldo, six
tiers of bands representing, from the base to the top,
*scenes from the life of Saint John the Baptist, stories of
Christ, of Joseph, of Genesis, Celestial Hierarchies* and
ornamental motifs.

*Facing page: the South Doors of the Baptistery, by Andrea Pisano,
with the Stories of the Baptist. This page, above: interior of the
Baptistery, and, to the right, the Tomb of the Anti-Pope John XXIII
designed by Michelozzo and Donatello.*

*Following two pages. Left: a view of the interior of the cupola of
the Baptistery with the arch of the scarsella and its mosaics. Right:
the octagon of the cupola completely lined with mosaic
decoration.*

Above, left: Madonna and Child by Arnolfo di Cambio, between S. Reparata, also by Arnolfo, and S. Zenobius, by assistants, inside the Museo dell'Opera del Duomo. Right: the statue of Boniface VIII by Arnolfo di Cambio.

Facing page, above: Donatello's choir-loft; below: Donatello's Magdalen between two prophets originally on Giotto's Campanile; the one on the left, Habacuc, has been nicknamed « Lo Zuccone » (Pumpkin head).

MUSEO DELL'OPERA DEL DUOMO

The museum is situated across from the apse of the Cathedral and contains works of art from the Duomo, the Campanile and the Baptistery. Over the entrance is the *Bust of Cosimo I* by Bandini. Inside are Romanesque sculpture, statues and remains of the original facade of the Duomo and the Baptistery. Works on the ground floor include the statues of the *Blessing Boniface VIII,* Arnolfo di Cambio's *Madonna and Child* and his *Madonna of the Nativity,* as well as Nanni di Banco's famous *St. Luke.* In an adjacent room *books, illuminated chorales* and *reliquaries.* On the first floor is the room with the *choir-loft,* by Luca della Robbia (1431-1438) with ten reliefs inspired by the joyous *Psalm of King David,* and Donatello's *choir-loft* (1433-1439), with a severe architectural layout inspired by classical antiquity. These two masterpieces in marble were removed from the Duomo in 1686 by Ferdinando de' Medici. The same room contains the statues which once stood on the Campanile, such as Donatello's figures of the prophets *Habacuc,* known as lo Zuccone (Pumpkin head), and *Jeremiah,* and Nanni di Bartolo's *Abraham and Isaac.* In the room to the left are to be found the original panels from Giotto's campanile, arranged in their original order. Outstanding examples by Andrea Pisano in the lower tier include the famous *Creation of Adam, Creation of Eve* and

Working of the Land; those in the upper tier are by the school of Pisano and by Alberto Arnoldi and depict the *Sacraments.* In the room to the right is the lovely *altar frontal* from the Baptistery, a magnificent example of Gothic goldwork with gilding and enamel, which was not completed until the Renaissance. Michelozzo, Verrocchio, Antonio del Pollaiolo and Bernardo Cennini all collaborated on this masterpieces.
On either side are statues of the *Virgin of the Annunciation* and the *Archangel Gabriel,* attributed to Jacopo della Quercia. Other examples of painting and sculpture which draw our attention in the museum, apart from Michelangelo's famous *Deposition,* include a noteworthy diptych with *Stories of Christ and the Madonna,* late 13th-century Byzantine school, and above all, halfway down the stairs, the *Magdalen,* an intense wooden statue by Donatello. The almost feverish execution and the material itself make this pathetically moving work seem real. The figure belongs to Donatello's last Florentine period (to be dated between 1435 and 1455) and recent restoration has restored it to its original coloring. Back on the ground floor it is of interest to study the *drawing* dating to the second half of the 16th century which depicts the original facade of the Duomo, before it was torn down in 1587, and the placing of the statues and architectonic decorations, many of which were salvaged and are on display in this same room.

MUSEUM DELL'OPERA DEL DUOMO

MICHELANGELO'S PIETÀ

This sculpture was originally in the Duomo. The central figure has been interpreted as a self-portrait of the artist. The Pietà was sculptured between 1550 and 1553 by Michelangelo for his chapel in S. Maria Maggiore in Rome. It remained, however, in the underground storerooms of S. Lorenzo until 1722 when it was transferred to the Duomo. It is probably one of Michelangelo's most dramatic pieces, an example of his painterly use of rough shaping (his famous « non-finito »). The restoration of Christ's left arm and the figure of the Magdalen were carried out by his pupil Tiberio Calcagni.

Left: wooden model of a project for the facade of the Duomo. Below, left: various hexagonal and rhomboid panels from Giotto's bell tower. Facing page: Michelangelo's Pietà.

Above: general view of the Piazza della Signoria.
Facing page: the Neptune Fountain.

PIAZZA DELLA SIGNORIA

One of the most scenographic squares in Italy was built and enlarged between the 13th and 14th centuries, thanks to the demolition of the palaces of the Uberti, Foraboschi and other Ghibelline families. The asymmetrical complex of the **Palazzo Vecchio**, on the northern side, dominates the square. To the right is the **Loggia dei Lanzi**, a late Gothic structure built by Benci di Cione and Simone Talenti (1376-82), which houses a group of important sculptures, including Cellini's famous *Perseus* and *Hercules and the Centaur* by Giambologna. To the left of

the building is the lively **Neptune Fountain** by Bartolomeo Ammannati and collaborators (1563-1575). Because of the enormous white mass of the sea god set in the center of the fountain on a chariot drawn by sea horses, the Florentines renamed the sculpture « il Biancone », the « White Giant », and the name has stuck. Particularly interesting are the wonderful bronze figures at the base. To one side stands the **Equestrian statue of Cosimo I** (1594) by Giambologna. The square is surrounded by interesting old palaces.

LOGGIA DEI LANZI

The Loggia of the Signoria, known as the loggia of Orcagna (he supposedly designed it) or of the Lanzi (with reference to the mercenary guards of the Grand Duke Cosimo I), was built by Benci da Cione and Simone Talenti (1376-1391) for the public assemblies of the Signoria. The airy elegance of the building is typically late Gothic. The fine relief panels above the piers depict allegorical figures of *Virtues,* executed between 1384 and 1389 on designs by Agnolo Gaddi. Two *lions* flank the entrance stairway: one is an example of classic art, the other is by Flaminio Vacca (1600). Various outstanding pieces of sculpture are sheltered in the loggia: on the left, Cellini's famous *Perseus* (1553); formerly on the right, the *Rape of the Sabines* by Giambologna of 1583 (now in the Galleria dell'Accademia); in the center, *Hercules and the Centaur,* also by Giambologna (1599); *Ajax with the Body of Patrocles,* a Hellenistic sculpture that has been reintegrated; and the *Rape of Polyxena* by Pio Fedi (1866). Six *statues of matrons* dating to Roman times are set against the back wall. A Latin inscription on the right wall, dating to 1750, refers to the substitution of the Florentine calendar (the beginning of the year on March 25th) with the normal calendar.

PERSEUS

This masterpiece in bronze by Benvenuto Cellini (1500-1571) is as splendid as it is famous. The artist signed the work on the strap that crosses the hero's chest in 1545-1554. Andromeda's liberator is shown just after he has cut off the Medusa's head. The features and the entire figure transmit the classic ideal of restrained force. The drama is over and the grave gesture (the hero's foot set on the monster's body) suggests achievement. According to tradition the complicated ornamentation of the winged helmet Perseus is wearing conceals a self-portrait of the artist. The bas-relief (a copy of the original now in the Bargello) with *Perseus liberating Andromeda* is in the pedestal where the refinement of execution and the decorative fantasy reveal Cellini's mastery as a goldsmith.

Facing page: views of the exterior and interior of the Loggia dei Lanzi. Right: Cellini's bronze Perseus.

COSIMO I DE' MEDICI GRAND DUKE OF TUSCANY

The equestrian statue, situated in the center of the square, represents Cosimo I de' Medici and was made by Giambologna in 1594. The fiercely proud Florentine nobleman astride his powerful steed gives an impression of the utmost composure. The bas-reliefs of the pedestal celebrate the chief events in the life of the first Grand Duke of Tuscany: the *Entry of Cosimo I in Siena, Pius V giving the grand-ducal insignia to Cosimo* and the *Tuscan Senate giving Cosimo the title of Duke of Florence*. The statue is situated not far from the Palazzo Vecchio, where Cosimo I went to live in 1537, when he was eighteen, just after the death of Alessandro, murdered by Lorenzino de' Medici. Before him, the Medici family had ruled Florence for a long time, ever since they had taken part in the struggle between the Guilds and the common people, siding with the latter.

PALAZZO VECCHIO

Begun in 1294 and intended as a palace-fortress for the residence of the Priors, Arnolfo di Cambio conceived of the building as a large squared block terminated by a row of crenellations. It is characterized by the powerful thrust of the *Tower* of 1310 (94 m. high) which rises from the Gallery. Externally the structure is in rusticated ashlars of *pietra forte* which lend the large building, divided into three floors and decorated with two-light openings inscribed in round-headed arches, a highly impressive air and a sense of austerity. Between 1343 and 1592 modifications and additions were made to Arnolfo's original nucleus, both inside and out (Cronaca, Vasari, Buontalenti all worked on it). To be noted on the facade under the arches of the gallery are the frescoes with the nine *coats of arms* of the city communes. The mechanism of the *clock* dates to 1667. On either side the doorway are marble *statues* to hold chains, with above them an inscription Cosimo I had set there in 1551. Near the left hand corner of the palace is the *Neptune Fountain* by Ammannati.

Left: the equestrian statue of Cosimo I dei Medici. Facing page: the imposing mass of the Palazzo Vecchio.

Facing page, above: the entrance to Palazzo Vecchio with Hercules and Cacus; below, left: the courtyard by Michelozzo with Verrocchio's Putto and, to the right, the copy of Michelangelo's David.

Above: the interior of the asymmetrical Salone dei Cinquecento, richly decorated with painting and sculpture.

PALAZZO VECCHIO

FACADE

Various statues are lined up in front of the Palazzo Vecchio, including a copy of Michelangelo's *David*, that replaced the original in 1873, and the group of *Hercules and Cacus* by Bandinelli. On the facade, above the door, there is a medallion with the monogram of Christ between two lions in a blue field, surmounted by a gable. The inscription « *Rex regum et Dominus dominantium* » was placed there in 1551 by order of Cosimo I, to replace the previous inscription, set there thirty years before.

PALAZZO VECCHIO

INTERIOR

After passing through **Michelozzo's Court**, with gilded stucco columns and frescoes by Vasari, and with Verrocchio's *Fountain with a Winged Putto holding a Fish* in the center, Vasari's broad staircase leads to the imposing **Salone dei Cinquecento**, and to the **Studiolo of Francesco I**, created by Vasari and full of *panels* painted

by Bronzino, Santi di Tito, Stradano, as well as bronze *statues* by Giambologna and Ammannati. Access to the **State Apartments** is also from the Salone dei Cinquecento. The numerous rooms full of paintings and frescoes include the **Hall of Leo X** (at present occupied by the Mayor and the City Councilors); the **Hall of Clement VII** with Vasari's famous fresco of the *Siege of Florence* with a detailed view of the l6th-century city; the **Hall of Giovanni dalle Bande Nere**, the **Halls of Cosimo the Elder**, **Lorenzo the Magnificent** and of **Cosimo I**.

SALONE DEI CINQUECENTO

The Salone dei Cinquecento (prepared to house the assemblies of the Consiglio Generale del Popolo after the Medicis had been expelled from Florence for the second time) is by il Cronaca, while the frescoes were entrusted to Vasari. The allegorical paintings on the ceiling and the walls narrate the triumphal *Return of Grand Duke Cosimo I to Florence*, illustrate the possessions of the *Medici Ducato* and the *Stories of the Conquest of Pisa and Siena*. The marble statues include, on the right hand wall, Michelangelo's striking *Genius of Victory*.

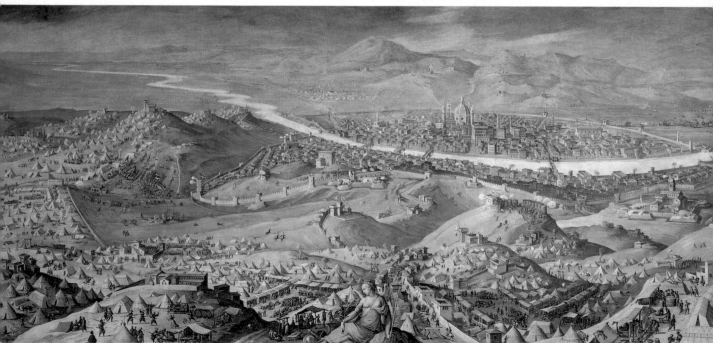

Facing page, above, left: Michelangelo's Youth conquering Brute Force; right: Hercules and Diomedes by Vincenzo de' Rossi; below: Vasari's fresco of the Siege of Florence in the Hall of Clement VII.

Above, left: the coffered ceiling of the Salone dei Cinquecento; right: Francesco I's Studiolo. Below: Vasari's painting of Giovanni dei Medici coming to the aid of Ravenna, in the Hall of Leo X.

Above, right: the original of Verrocchio's putto with a fish. Left: the Camera Verde of Eleonor of Toledo's private apartments. Below, right: Donatello's Judith; left: the Cappella dei Priori.

SALA DEI GIGLI

Of particular note among the State Apartments, after Vasari's **Apartment of Eleonora of Toledo** and the **Audience Hall**, is the **Sala dei Gigli**, which receives its name from the decorations of golden fleur de lis on a blue ground (*ceiling* by Giuliano da Maiano and Francione). The marble *doorway* that leads to the Audience hall is particularly fine. On the walls of the hall is a large *fresco* by Domenico Ghirlandaio.

JUDITH: A RESTORED WORK OF ART

For centuries Donatello's masterpiece, Judith, which has recently been restored by the Opificio delle Pietre Dure (it took two years to complete the work), stood in the Piazza della Signoria. The bronze sculpture was removed from its original site in 1980 and transferred to the Audience Hall in Palazzo Vecchio. In 1986 it was once more moved so that it could be restored. Today the statue is once more there for the public to enjoy in all its splendid luminous forms inside the Palazzo in the large Sala dei Gigli where it can be perfectly preserved and protected from the elements.

Above: the interior of the Sala dei Gigli and, to the right, Donatello's Judith.

Above: the Bargello with the tower of the Volognana which counterbalances the Campanile of the Badia. Facing page: two views of the Bargello courtyard with the loggia.

PALAZZO DEL BARGELLO

The Palazzo del Bargello is like a fortress with powerful embattlements (the **Volognana**) surmounting the austere facade. It was built in 1255 as the seat of the Capitano del Popolo, and the Podestà and the Consiglio di Giustizia were then housed there. In 1574 it became the living quarters for the Bargello (Captain of Justice, or chief of police). The exterior, articulated by cornices, has lintelled windows in the lower part and two-light openings or simple windows further up. The crenellation at the top juts out supported on small arches and corbels. The interior is centered around a **courtyard** with porticoes on three sides, with piers and arcading. A picturesque **covered staircase**, built in the l4th century by Neri di Fioravante, leads to the upper **loggia**, by Tone di Giovanni (1319). The walls of the courtyard are covered with dozens of *coats of arms* of the various Podestà and Giudici di Ruota. Since 1859 the place has been the site of the **Museo Nazionale** (one of the most important in the world) which contains

Renaissance sculpture and masterpieces of the minor arts from varying periods.

MUSEO NAZIONALE DEL BARGELLO

The enormous **Entrance hall** on piers with solid vaulting has heraldic decorations on the walls with the coats of arms of the podestà (13th-14th cent.).
From here to the scenographic **Courtyard** which is irregular and unique. The coats of arms of many podestà are here and, under the portico, the picturesque insignia of the quarters and the districts into which the city was once divided. Various 16th-century *statues* set against the walls are by Bandinelli, Ammannati, Giambologna and Danti.
The courtyard leads to a **Hall** with a collection of 14th-century sculpture, including Tino da Camaino's *Madonna and Child with Angel,* a meditating *Madonna and Child* of Venetian school, the *base of a holy water stoup* by Nicola Pisano and a *Madonna between St. Peter and St. Paul* by Paolo di Giovanni (circa 1328). In the Room close to the open staircase are important works by Michelangelo: the *Bacchus* (1470), an early work of great power despite the softness of form, the *Pitti Tondo,* with the Madonna teaching Jesus and St. John to read (1504), the *David* or

Above: the hall on the lower floor of the Bargello with the collection of Renaissance sculpture. Left: the bust of Cosimo I by Cellini. Facing page, above: Leda and the Swan by Ammannati; below, left: a marble bust of Cosimo I by Baccio Bandinelli, and, to the right, Michelangelo's Brutus.

Apollo (1530), the *Brutus* (1540). There are also works by Ammannati, Giambologna (including his famous Mercury of 1564) Tribolo, Danti, Francavilla and Sansovino who made a *Bacchus* of his own to compete with Michelangelo's. The bronze *bust of Cosimo I* by Cellini, made for Portoferraio in Elba and brought back in 1781, is also in the same room.

The *Open Staircase,* leads to the **Loggia**, ornamented with various works by other 16th-century artists.

The first room to the right, once the Salone del Consiglio Generale, is now the **Donatello Room** and contains many of his works such as the *St. George* (1416) with its self-contained energy, made for the niche in Orsanmichele, the young *St. John,* slender and mystical, the marble *David* (1408) and the bronze *David,* the first delicate Renaissance nude made around 1430. Also by Donatello are the *Marzocco,* the symbol of the city, and the lively bronze *Amor-Attis,* revealing a classic influence. In addition to works by Luca della Robbia, Ghiberti, Vecchietta and Agostino di Duccio, the room also contains the *trial panels* which Ghiberti and Brunelleschi made in 1402 for the competition (there were six contestants) for the second doors of the Florentine Baptistery.

Access to the **Collection of Decorative Arts,** mostly based on the donation of the Carrand Collections, is from the hall. *Goldwork* and *enamels* from the Middle Ages to the 16th century, *seals* and various metal objects are in the **Salone del Podestà**.

In the adjacent **Cappella del Podestà**, where those

Above, left: the Pitti Tondo by Michelangelo; right: the bust of Michelangelo by Daniele da Volterra; below, left: the David or Apollo by Michelangelo. Facing page, above left: Bacchus by Sansovino, done in competition with Michelangelo's Bacchus (on the right). Below, left: the model for Cellini's Perseus, and, on the right, Giambologna's Mercury.

condemned to death passed their last hours, there are Giottesque frescoes with *Paradise, Hell* and *Stories of the Saints*. The floor is completed by the **Sala degli Avori**, with rare carvings from the ancient period to the 15th century; the **Sala delle Oreficerie**, with numerous works of sacred art, and the **Sala delle Majoliche**.

The second floor of the Bargello contains other rooms dedicated to great artists: the first, known as the **Giovanni della Robbia Room**, contains a number of the master's sculptures including the predella with Christ and Saints, St. Dominic, the Pietà and the Annunciation.

The following **Andrea della Robbia Room** houses the *Madonna degli Architetti* and other works in glazed terracotta. In the **Verrocchio Room** are the *Resurrection*, the *bust of a young woman*, the *Madonna and Child*, the bronze *David* and other works by the master as well as various *busts* and sculpture by Mino da Fiesole and the group of *Hercules and Antaeus* by Pollaiolo, with the vibrating force of the two struggling figures. Other bronze sculpture is in the **Sala dei Bronzetti** with the *mantelpiece of Casa Borgherini* by Benedetto da Rovezzano; the **Sala delle Armi** houses military paraphernalia from the Middle Ages to the 17th century. The museum is completed by the **Sala della Torre** with tapestries and the **Medagliere Mediceo** with works by artists such as Pisanello, Cellini, Michelozzo and others.

Facing page: two views of S. Croce. Above: the interior of the basilica; right: the marble pulpit by Benedetto da Maiano.

CHURCH OF S. CROCE

This monument is truly unique, not only for the purity of the Gothic style, but also for the famous works of art it contains and its historical importance. The Basilica of Santa Croce, one of the largest churches in the city, is attributed to the genius of Arnolfo di Cambio who seems to have begun work in 1294. Work continued into the second half of the 14th century but the church was not consecrated until 1443. The facade with its three gables dates to the 19th century (project by N. Matas) and the **campanile** in Gothic style also dates to this period (1847, project by G. Baccani). A portico of airy arches runs along the left flank and shelters the 14th-century *tomb of Francesco Pazzi*. On the right side of the church are the **Cloisters**, with the **Pazzi Chapel** in the background, and the **Museo dell'Opera di S. Croce**. The imposing interior has a nave and two side aisles separated by slender octagonal piers from which spring spacious pointed arches with a double molding. The beauty of the Church has been partially obfuscated by 16th-century remodelling. The floor is covered with old tombstones for the entire length of the nave which has a trussed timber ceiling. The transept has a number of chapels, including the **Cappella Maggiore** with the *Legend of the Holy Cross* (1380) by Agnolo Gaddi. On the altar is Gerini's polyptych with the *Madonna and Saints* and, above, the *Crucifix* of the school

GALILAEVS GALILEIVS PATRIC. FLOR.
GEOMETRIAE ASTRONOMIAE PHILOSOPHIAE MAXIMVS RESTITVTOR
NVLLI AETATIS SVAE COMPARANDVS
HIC BENE QVIESCAT
VIX. A. LXXVIII. OBIIT. A. CIƆ IƆ C. XXXXI.
CVRANTIBVS AETERNVM PRIMVM ELOVS
XVIRI PATRICIIS SACRAE HVIVS AEDIS PRAEFECTI
MONVMENTVM A VINCENTIO VIVIANO MAGISTRI CINERI SVEIVE SIBIVL
TESTAMENTO EI.
HERES IO. BAPT. CLEMENS NELLIN KL BAPT. SENATORIS E.
LVBENTI ANIMO ABSOLVIT.
AN. CIƆ IƆCCXXXVII.

Facing page, above, left: funeral monument to Michelangelo; right: funeral monument to Galileo Galilei. Below: the Tabernacle of the Annunciation with a detail of the Angel, by Donatello. This page, above, left: funeral monument to Alfieri, the Italian poet, and, on the right, to Machiavelli. Below: the funeral monument to Dante Alighieri.

of Giotto. A *Deposition from the Cross* (cartoon by Lorenzo Ghiberti) in stained glass can be admired on the interior facade. Below to the right is the *Monument to Gino Capponi* (1070), and to the left that to *G. B. Niccolini* (1883). A splendid marble *pulpit* by Benedetto da Maiano (1472-76) stands in the nave. To be noted in the right aisle, at the first altar, is a *Crucifixion* by Santi di Tito (1579); on the first pier is the famous bas-relief by Antonio Rossellino (1478) of the *Madonna del Latte*. The *stained-glass windows* date to the 14th century. The most famous *funeral monuments* are along the walls of the right aisle. These include the monument to *Dante Alighieri* by Ricci (1829); to *Michelangelo,* by Vasari (1579); to *Alfieri,* by Canova (1803); to *Machiavelli,* by I. Spinazzi (1787). Fragments of *frescoes* by Orcagna are to be seen behind the fourth altar and further on is Domenico Veneziano's fine fresco (1450) of *St. John the Baptist and St. Francis.* Next comes the tabernacle in *pietra serena* by Donatello and Michelozzo with the *Annunciation* (1435 c.) by Donatello. and then the *Tomb of Leonardo Bruni* by Bernardo Rossellino, the *funeral monument to Rossini* and the one to Foscolo. The right arm of the transept contains the **Castellani Chapel** superbly frescoed by Agnolo Gaddi (1385) with *Stories of the Saints.* On the altar a *Crucifix* by Gerini.

Opposite, the Cappella Maggiore, in Santa Croce. On this pag(e?)
(above), a fresco by Giotto: the funeral of St. Francis, in the B(ardi?)
Chapel; (left), a view of the chapel with a panel painting of
St. Francis, by an anonymous master of the 13th century.

50

At the end of the transept is the **Baroncelli Chapel**, with the splendid Gothic *tomb* of the Baroncelli family and a lunette with a *Madonna* by Taddeo Gaddi. The frescoes on the walls with *Stories of Mary* are also by Gaddi and the *Madonna of the Girdle* is by Bastiano Mainardi (1490). The *Coronation of the Virgin* on the altar is by Giotto. Michelozzo's portal leads to the **Sacristy**, with the **Rinuccini Chapel**, frescoed with *Stories of the Magdalen and the Virgin* by Giovanni da Milano. The fine *altarpiece* is by Giovanni del Biondo (1379). Michelozzo's **Medici Chapel**, built for Cosimo the Elder, is at the back. It contains a magnificent *bas-relief* by Donatello and various works by the Della Robbias. Various chapels (14th-cent.) with important works open off the central zone of the transept. These include the **Velluti Chapel** with *Stories of St. Michael Archangel,* perhaps by Cimabue; the **Chapels of the Peruzzi and the Bardi** families frescoed by Giotto with *Stories of St. John the Evangelist* (1320) and *Stories of St. Francis* (1318); the **Tosinghi Chapel** with the *Assumption in Heaven,* also by Giotto; the **Pulci Chapel** with frescoes by Bernardo Daddi. Of particular note in the left aisle is the *Marsuppini Sepulcher* by Desiderio da Settignano.

Facing page: the Baroncelli Chapel. This page, above, right: Giotto's panel of the Coronation of the Virgin, in the same chapel; below: the Castellani Chapel with the Crucifix by Niccolò di Pietro Gerini.

*Above: the Sacristy with the Rinuccini Chapel;
below: the Pazzi Chapel.*

PAZZI CHAPEL AND MUSEO DI S. CROCE

At the back of the Basilica's **First Cloister** is the **Pazzi Chapel**, a daring example of Brunelleschi's genius, begun in 1443. The decorations are by Desiderio da Settignano, Luca della Robbia, Giuliano da Maiano. A pronaos or porch on Corinthian columns precedes the chapel. The cylindrical dome, with a conical roof and a round lantern, was finished in 1461. The interior is a jewel of Renaissance harmony with its white walls articulated by the grey stone pilaster strips. The **Museo dell'Opera di S. Croce** has been installed in the **Refectory**, to the right of the **Cloister**.

Above: the Refectory of S. Croce. Below, left: Cimabue's Crucifix and, on the right, a Della Robbian tabernacle in the Museum of S. Croce.

SANT E PATER · BARTOL OMEE · ORA · PR ONOBIS

UFFIZI

The gallery of the Uffizi is the most famous picture gallery in Italy and one of the best known in the world. It furnishes a complete panorama of the various schools of Florentine painting, represented by important works and authentic masterpieces. It also includes numerous collections of other Italian schools (particularly the Venetian) and a fine group of Flemish paintings, as well as the famous collections of self-portraits. To be noted also are the antique statues and an extensive collection of tapestries. The Uffizi was commissioned from Giorgio Vasari by the Medicis as administrative and judicial offices (thence the name). Begun in 1560 and finished twenty years later, the two wings with a loggiato at the bottom are connected by a third wing with arches along the Arno. On either side of the central courtyard powerful piers contain niches with 19th-century statues of illustrious Tuscans, while the upper floors of the building have windows (1st floor) and a running loggia (2nd floor). In addition to the **Gallery**, which is on the second floor, the building houses the **State Archives** which contain rare documents from the city's history. On the ground floor note should be taken of the remains of the Romanesque church of **San Piero Scheraggio** (brought to light and restored in 1971) with fine frescoes by Andrea del Castagno. On the first floor is the **Gabinetto dei Disegni e delle Stampe** (Drawing and Print Cabinet), an imposing

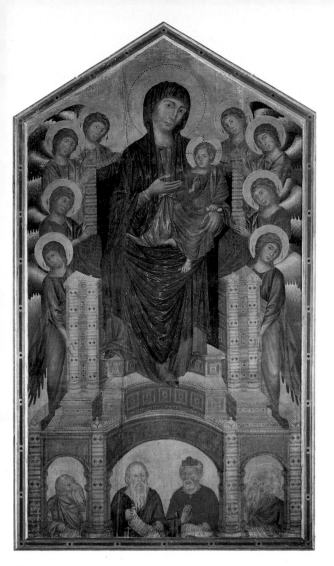

Facing page, above: the side of the Uffizi overlooking the Arno. Below: the courtyard of the Uffizi.

Above, left: Santa Trinita Madonna, by Cimabue; right: Ognissanti Madonna, by Giotto. Below: the panel with Christ the Redeemer and four Saints, by Meliore di Jacopo.

Above: the San Pancrazio Polyptych, by Bernardo Daddi. Left: The Annunciation, by Simone Martini.

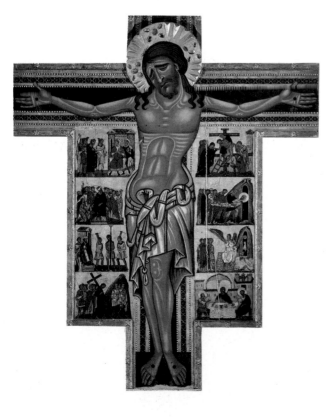

Above, left: Madonna and Child with Angels, by Pietro Lorenzetti.
Right: Presentation in the Temple, by Ambrogio Lorenzetti.
Left: Crucifix with stories from the Passion, by the Master of the
Dardi Saint Francis.

collection begun in the 17th century at the behest of
Cardinal Leopoldo de' Medici.
The visit to the Gallery begins on the second floor. This
great museum did not become public patrimony until
1737, a gift of Anna Maria Ludovica de' Medici, the last
of this prestigious family. The gallery consists of 45 rooms
divided into sections.

57

Above: The Duke and Duchess of Urbino, by Piero della Francesca. Right: Madonna and Child with Saints, by Ghirlandaio.

Above: Magnificat Madonna, by Botticelli. Facing page, above:
Primavera; below: Birth of Venus, both by Botticelli.

Above: the Portinari tryptyc by Hugo van der Goes. Left: The Adoration of the Magi by Gentile da Fabriano.

Above: Holy Family (Doni Tondo), by Michelangelo.

*Above, left: Cosimo the Elder, by
Pontormo. Right: Madonna and Child, by
Giulio Romano. Left: Slaughter of the
Innocents, by Daniele da Volterra. Facing
page, above: Venus and Cupid, by
Alessandro Allori; below: Henriette of
France as Flora, by Jean Marc Nattier.*

Above: Ponte Vecchio on the downstream side of the Arno. Left: the Bust of Cellini in the middle of the bridge. Facing page, above: the upstream side of the bridge and, below, a detail of some of the workshops on the bridge and the arches which support Vasari's Corridor.

BRIDGES OF FLORENCE AND THE PONTE VECCHIO

Currently there are ten Florentine bridges, but until 1957 there were six, modified in the course of the centuries and all, except the Ponte Vecchio, rebuilt after their destruction in 1944 by mines. The **Ponte Vecchio** is the oldest bridge in the city, not only because it is the only one which survived, but also because it stands on the site of at least three precedent bridges: one in Roman times, the one that was ruined in 1117, and the one destroyed when the Arno flooded in 1333. The bridge so greatly admired now was built by Neri di Fioravante (1345), a solid but elegant structure with three arches. It is characterized by the small houses that line both sides of the bridge. In the 14th century these rows of buildings had a much more regular appearance but as time went by various changes and additions led to their current picturesque variety. At about the center of the span over the river, the buildings are interrupted by a widening of the roadway, thus furnishing a fine view of the Arno and the other bridges.

Vasari's Corridor passes along over the bridge, above the buildings. It allowed Cosimo I to reach Palazzo Pitti from Palazzo Vecchio without running any risks. Ever since the 16th century the shops on the bridge have been the laboratory-shops of goldsmiths (previously some of them were butcher shops).

The second Florentine bridge was the **Ponte Nuovo** or

Ponte alla Carraia (1220), which served for the heavy traffic of the time. It was also reconstructed after the floods of 1274 and 1333, and then once more after it fell in 1944. The third bridge was the **Ponte alle Grazie** (1237), so-called because of a chapel dedicated to the Madonna delle Grazie. What we see now is post-war. The fourth bridge is the **Ponte S. Trinita**, a masterpiece by Ammannati (1567-70); Michelangelo supervised the project. It replaced previous bridges (the earliest dated to 1257) which had been carried away by the floods. At the beginning and end of the bridge are the statues of the *Four Seasons* (set there in 1608). The present bridge is the result of a reconstruction carried out « as it was and where it was » in the 1950s, after it had been destroyed in the war. The other two bridges date to the 19th century — the one of **S. Niccolò** and the one at the Cascine (which was originally a suspended bridge), rebaptized in 1928 **Ponte alla Vittoria**. The **Ponte Vespucci** was inaugurated in 1957. It is the first modern bridge and the seventh in the series. In 1969 **Ponte Giovanni da Verrazzano** was added and, recently, the **Viaduct of the Indian**, beyond the Cascine, and the one of **Varlungo**.

THE MANNELLI TOWER

The Mannelli tower belonged to the Manelli family, in origin Ghibelline, that later split into two factions: Guelph and Ghibelline. Luckily this building was saved from demolition. Vasari's Corridor, the building of which was ordered by Cosimo I, was to have passed through it. After the protests of Mannelli, the Grand Duke left the building intact. We can still see it on the Oltrarno side of the Ponte Vecchio.

Left: the Mannelli Tower. Below: Ponte Vecchio and its shops. Facing page, above: Ponte S. Trinita and Ponte Vecchio; below: Ponte S. Trinita on the upstream side.

BRIDGE AND SQUARE OF SANTA TRINITA

The **Bridge of Santa Trinita** is adorned with the statues of *Spring* and *Summer* on the northern side towards the center (opposite; left, below). Walking past **Ferroni Palace** (opposite, above) we reach **Piazza Santa Trinita** (opposite; right, below), adorned in the center with the **Column of Justice**, a Roman shaft originally from the Baths of Caracalla with the statue of Justice on the top.

PIAZZA DELLA REPUBBLICA

What was once the ancient Roman forum where the *cardo* and the *decumanus* crossed, was the lively center of the Mercato Vecchio (Old Market) in medieval times. It acquired its present aspect, anonymous and in Piedmontese style, when the center of Florence was torn down in 1887, so lamentable in many ways. The old towers and houses, the historical Hebrew ghetto, churches, shops and open-air markets gave way to the palaces, cafés, and the enormous *arcade* that leads to the Via Strozzi, dedicated together with the square to Vittorio Emanuele II.

PALAZZO STROZZI

This typical example of a Renaissance palace was designed by Benedetto da Maiano in 1489 (work continued under various superintendents until 1538). The broad portal with a rusticated arch and the rectangular windows are set into the lower part in *pietra forte*. The upper part, attributed to il Cronaca, is articulated by two denticular cornices of classic taste, while a large cornice crowns the building. The windows are two-light openings.

Right: Palazzo Strozzi. Below: Piazza della Repubblica.

CHURCH OF ORSANMICHELE

Once a loggia used as a grain market (built by Arnolfo di Cambio, 1290), it was destroyed in a fire in 1304. Rebuilt in 1337 (the work of Francesco Talenti, Neri di Fioravante and Neri di Cione), between 1380 and 1404 the structure was transformed into a church. The austere lines of the large cubic building (with the arcading serving as a base) are softened by the late Gothic marble decoration. The upper part is in *pietra forte* with two tiers of large two-light openings. Niches and tabernacles with statues are set into the outer walls (particularly famous are Ghiberti's *St. John the Baptist,* 1414-16; Verrocchio's *St. Thomas,* 1464-83; Nanni di Banco's *Four Crowned Martyrs,* 1408; the copy of Donatello's *St. George,* 1416). Inside the church is the imposing *Tabernacle* by Orcagna, in flamboyant Gothic style (1355-59).

Opposite (above), the Loggia del Mercato Nuovo, constructed in the middle of the 16th century by Giovan Battista del Tasso. In the niches: 17th century statues representing illustrious Florentines of the past.

Opposite (below). the square construction of which the church of Orsanmichele occupies the ground floor; on this page (above), Orcagna's tabernacle and (below) the interior of Orsanmichele.

Above: the facade of S. Maria Novella. Left: one of the obelisks in the piazza. Facing page: two views of the Spanish Chapel.

CHURCH OF. S. MARIA NOVELLA

The Dominican friars, Sisto da Firenze and Ristoro da Campi, began to build the church in 1246 on the site of the 10th-century Dominican oratory of S. Maria delle Vigne. The nave and aisles went up in 1279 and the building was finished in the middle of the 14th century with the **campanile** and the **Sacristy** by Jacopo Talenti. The marvelous facade was remodelled between 1456 and 1470 by Leon Battista Alberti (the original facade was early 14th century) who created the splendid portal and everything above it, articulated in inlaid squares and bordered by the *heraldic sails* of the Rucellai family who commissioned the work. Two large reversed volutes tie the lateral masses together with those in the center, articulated by four engaged pilasters and terminating in a triangular pediment. The interior is divided into a nave and two aisles by compound piers with pointed arches, and 16th-century renovation.

CHURCH OF S. MARIA NOVELLA

INTERIOR
The church houses numerous works from the 14th to the 16th centuries. Of particular note are the *Monument to the Beata Villana* by Rossellino (1451); the *Bust of St. Antoninus* (in terra cotta) and the *Tomb of the Bishop of Fiesole* by Tino da Camaino; Ghiberti's lovely *tombstone for Leonardo Dati* (1423); the *Tomb of Filippo Strozzi* by Benedetto da Maiano 1491); Vasari's *Madonna of the Rosary* (1568); the *Miracle of Jesus* by Bronzino. Be sure

to stop for a while in the **Cappella Maggiore** (or Tornabuoni Chapel), with a fine bronze *Crucifix* by Giambologna on the altar and frescoes with the *Stories of St. John the Baptist* and *Stories of the Madonna* by Domenico Ghirlandaio, late 15th cent.); the **Gondi Chapel**, by Giuliano da Sangallo, with fragments of .*frescoes* by 13th-century Greek painters on the vault and Brunelleschi's famous *Crucifix* on the back wall; the **Cappella Strozzi di Mantova**, with frescoes of the *Last Judgement* on the back wall, *Hell* on the right wall and *Paradise* on the left, by Nardo di Cione or Orcagna. The gate to the left of the facade leads to the **First Cloister**, in Romanesque style (1350) frescoed with *Scenes from the Old Testament* by Paolo Uccello (now in the **Refectory**). From here, through the **Chiostrino dei Morti**, one arrives at the **Chiostro Grande**, with more than fifty arches and completely lined with frescoes by Florentine masters of the 15th and 16th centuries (generally not open to the public since it is now used by the armed forces).

SPANISH CHAPEL

The old *Chapter Hall* of the convent can be reached through the portal on the north side of the **First Cloister** (Chiostro Verde). Built by Jacopo Talenti (1359), in 1540 Eleonora of Toledo, Cosimo I's wife, took it over as her private chapel for the religious services of her court. It is completely lined with frescoes by Andrea di Bonaiuto (mid-14th cent.) which depict scenes inspired by the *Mirror of True Penitance* by the prior Jacopo Passavanti, exemplary *apologia* of the Dominican rule of St. Dominic and St. Thomas of Aquinas.

Facing page, above: the two-color arcading enclosing the left side of S. Maria Novella; below: the Chiostro Grande. This page: two details of the Spanish Chapel.

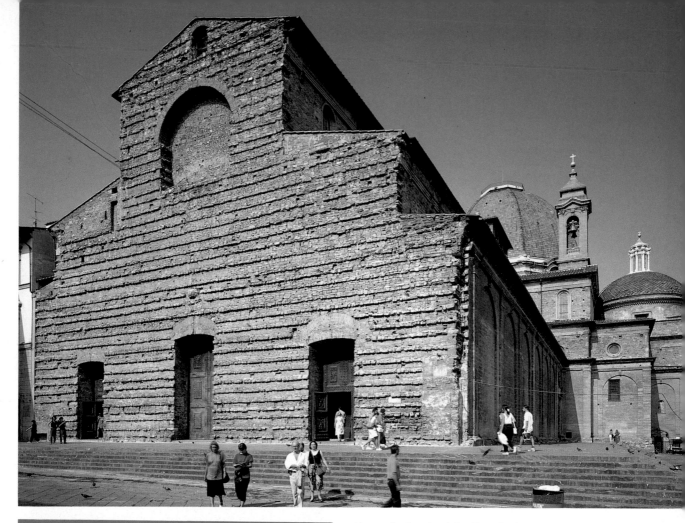

Above: the facade of the Church of S. Lorenzo. Left: the Cloister. Facing page, above: the interior of the church, and, below, one of the two bronze pulpits by Donatello.

CHURCH OF S. LORENZO

This is the oldest church in the city (consecrated by St. Ambrose in 393) and it was rebuilt along Romanesque lines in 1060. What we see now is Brunelleschi's adaptation of 1423. The facade, magnificent and moving in its bareness, was supposed to be faced with marble (Michelangelo's project was never carried out). Of particular note inside, among others, are Donatello's two *bronze pulpits and his choir-loft,* as well as the **Old Sacristy**, Brunelleschi's first work (1419-28).

MEDICI CHAPELS

The large complex, containing the tombs of the Medici, is just behind the Church of San Lorenzo. Various rooms and the vault are in common. From the entrance vestibule we enter a vast, low room, created by Buontalenti, where we can find the *tombs of Donatello, Cosimo the Elder, members of the Lorraine dynasty* as well as other grand-ducal tombs. The staircase leads to the large **Chapel of the Princes**, created and begun by Nigetti (with additional touches by Buontalenti) in 1602; it was finished in the eighteenth century. The interior is octagonal in shape, completely clad in pietradura and marble in line with the Baroque taste; above the base with *16 coats-of-arms* of the grand-ducal cities, there are *six sarcophagi* of the grand dukes *Cosimo III, Francesco I, Cosimo I, Ferdinando I, Cosimo II, Ferdinando II,* two of which have statues of the *Grand Dukes* by Tacca. A corridor leads from the Chapel of the Princes to the **New Sacristy**.

Left: the cupola of the Chapel of the Princes. Below: a view of the animated Borgo S. Lorenzo. Facing page, above: the interior of the cupola of the Chapel of the Princes, and, below, the altar.

SACRESTIA NUOVA

The **New Sacristy**, entered from the **Medici Chapels**, stands near the right transept of the **Basilica of S. Lorenzo**. Created by Michelangelo (1520), it overturns Brunelleschi's concept of restrained balance with the dynamic rhythms of its decoration. The Sacristy contains Michelangelo's *Medici Tombs*, that of *Giuliano*, duke of Nemours, and of *Lorenzo*, duke of Urbino. The figures of *Day* and *Night* watch over the tomb of Giuliano and *Dusk* and *Dawn* over that of Lorenzo.

This page: the coats of arms of Florence, Pisa, and Siena inlaid in stone on the walls of the Chapel of the Princes. Facing page: details of Michelangelo's figures in the New Sacristy. Above, left: the tomb of Giuliano, duke of Nemours; right: the tomb of Lorenzo, duke of Urbino; below: the Madonna and Child between Saints Cosmas and Damian.

Facing each other on the following pages are, above, Night and Day, and below, Dusk and Dawn, works by Michelangelo set on the tombs of the two Medici dukes.

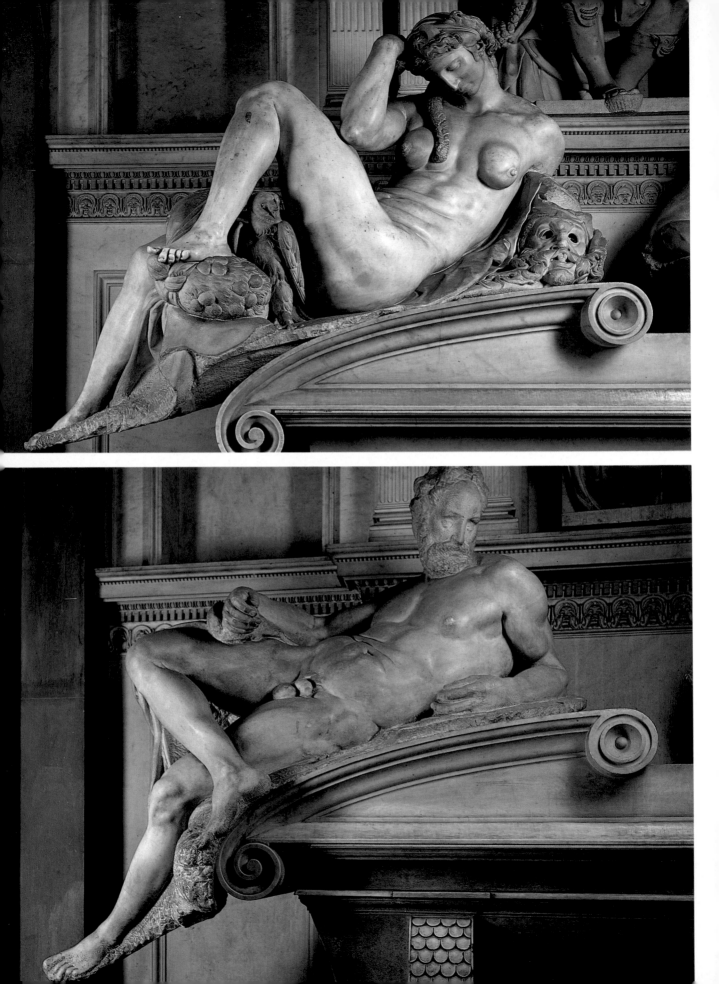

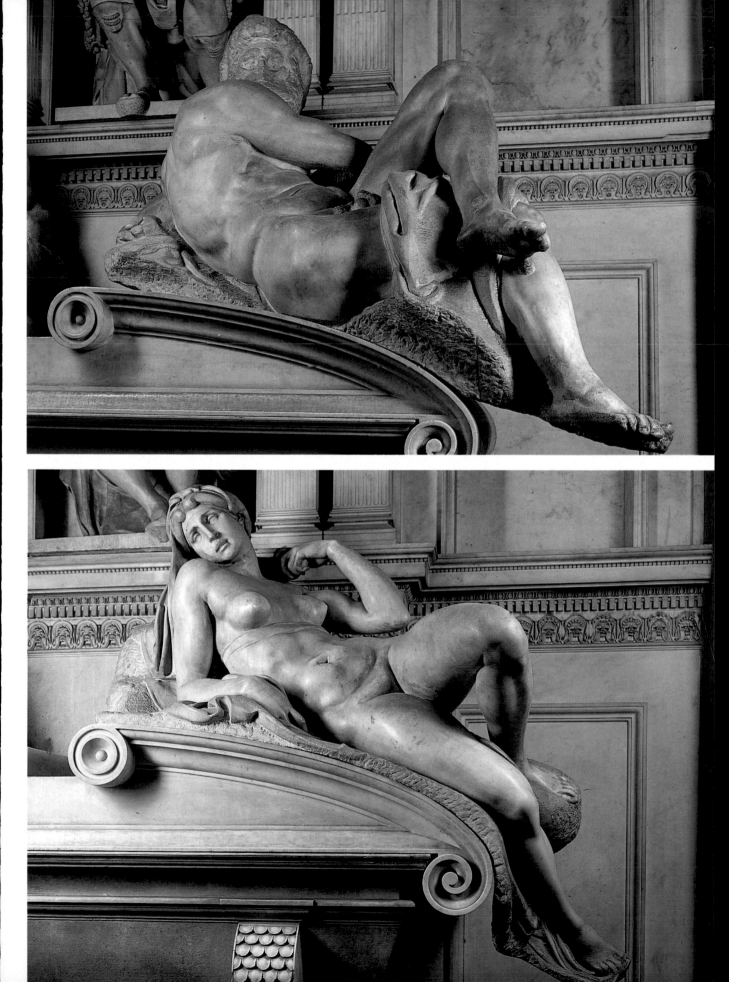

PALAZZO MEDICI-RICCARDI

This is the palace Cosimo the Elder had built for himself and his family. The work of Michelozzo (1444-1464), it is a model of the Renaissance upper-class dwelling. In 1517 the open loggia on the ground floor was walled up and the pedimented *windows* attributed to Michelangelo were added. In 1655 it was acquired by the Riccardi family who added on to the facade and the whole building, thus altering the original aspect. Outside, as the facade rises, the pronounced rustication of the ground floor passes to a smooth rustication in finely fitted flat slabs on the uppermost floor. The two-light windows have a small column topped by a roundel. A cornice on corbels, classical in style, runs along the top of the building. The palace, which once belonged to Lorenzo the Magnificent and is now the seat of the Prefecture, also contains the famous frescoes by Benozzo Gozzoli of the *Arrival of the Magi in Bethlehem* in its **Chapel** (also by Michelozzo). Painted in 1459-60, the fresco portrays the personages present at the Council of Florence in 1439 (recognizable are John VII, Lorenzo, Piero the Gouty with his daughters, Galeazzo Maria Sforza, Sigismondo Malatesta, as well as Benozzo himself and his master, Fra Angelico). Of particular note too is the **Courtyard** of the palace, with the porticoes set under a tier of two-light openings and a loggia, decorated with 15th-century *graffiti* by Maso di Bartolomeo and *medallions* by Bertoldo.

Facing page, above, left: Palazzo Medici Riccardi; right: the Room of Luca Giordano. Below and on this page, details of the Chapel in the Palazzo with frescoes by Benozzo Gozzoli depicting the Arrival of the Magi in Bethlehem.

Above: the equestrian statue of Ferdinando I dei Medici in front of the Ospedale degli Innocenti. Below, left: one of the Fountains by Tacca.

PIAZZA SS. ANNUNZIATA

After leaving the **Church of the SS. Annunziata**, to the left is the complex of the **Ospedale degli Innocenti** (designed by Brunelleschi and finished by F. Luna in 1445). The facade presents a lovely portico of nine arches decorated with polychrome terra-cotta roundels of *babes in swaddling clothes* (it was a foundling home) by Andrea della Robbia (1463). Inside is a magnificent **Courtyard** and the first floor houses the **Collection of detached frescoes** and the **Gallery of the Hospital**. Across the square, opposite the Ospedale is the **Portico of the Confraternità dei Servi di Maria**, built by Sangallo the Elder and Baccio d'Agnolo (1516-25) in imitation of Brunelleschi's portico. The *equestrian statue of Ferdinando de' Medici* stands at the center of the square. It is practically a twin to the one of Cosimo I in the Piazza della Signoria and was also by Giambologna although Tacca finished it (1608). The two *Fountains* symmetrically placed at the sides of the square are also by Tacca. They date to 1629 and were made for the port of Livorno.

Above: the facade of the Church of SS. Annunziata. Right: the Chiostro dei Voti within the complex.

CHURCH OF THE SS. ANNUNZIATA

Originally an oratory (1250) of the Order of the Servi di Maria, the building stood outside the second circle of city walls. Between 1444 and 1481 Michelozzo, Pagno Portinari and Antonio Manetti (with suggestions from L. B. Alberti) remodelled it into its present form. The facade has a portico on Corinthian columns. The central portal leads to the **Chiostrino dei Voti** (1447), a particularly scenographic space with lunettes frescoed by Rosso Fiorentino, Pontormo, Andrea del Sarto (1511-13). The interior, remodelled in the middle of the 17th century, has a single large nave with the arched openings of the chapels set on either side. To be noted is Volterrano's magnificent coffered *ceiling* (1664). Entrance to the **Chiostro dei Morti** (1453) with *frescoes* by Poccetti is to the left of the transept.

Above: detail of the head of Michelangelo's David. Facing page: Michelangelo's sculpture in the Tribune of the Accademia.

GALLERIA DELL'ACCADEMIA

The Gallery houses an extremely important collection of sculpture by Michelangelo. The room that leads to the tribune, hung with tapestries, contains the *Palestrina Pietà*, whose attribution to Michelangelo is controversial, the unfinished *St. Matthew,* made for the Florentine cathedral, and the four « *Prisons* » (or slaves) which were meant for the tomb of Julius II in St. Peter's in Rome, which was never finished, like these male figures who seem to be trying to free themselves from the marble grip.

At the center of the spacious **Tribune** is the original of the *David* (1501-4) commissioned from the great sculptor to replace Donatello's *Judith* on the balustrade of the Palazzo dei Priori. The room also contains an important collection of *paintings* of the Tuscan school of the 13th and 14th centuries.

Three small rooms are to the right of the *Tribune* and contain various *shrines* attributed to Bernardo Daddi and a fine *Pietà* by Giovanni da Milano. To the left another series of **three small rooms** which contain works by famous masters of the 14th century: of note are a fine *Polyptych* by Andrea Orcagna, and two series of panels representing *Scenes from the Life of Christ* and *Scenes from the Life of St. Francis,* by Taddeo Gaddi. To the left of the Tribune there is another large **hall** containing works of the Florentine 15th century, including Lorenzo Monaco's *Annunciation,* Filippino Lippi's *St. John the Baptist and the Magdalen,* the *Madonna of the Sea,* attributed either to Botticelli or Filippino Lippi, and a fine *panel from a wedding chest,* known as the *Adimari wedding chest,* by an unknown Florentine painter of the 15th century.

Facing page, above: three of Michelangelo's « Prisons »; below,
left to right: a « Prison », St. Matthew, and the Palestrina Pietà.
Above: the room in the Galleria dell'Accademia with the Rape of
the Sabines by Giambologna. Right: the Assumption and Saints
by Perugino.

Left: a 14th-century panel with the Madonna and Child.
Right: Botticelli's Madonna of the Sea. Below: the panel
on the front of the Adimari wedding chest.

Facing page, above: the Cloister of S. Marco; below: the
Room of the Hospice with works by Fra Angelico.

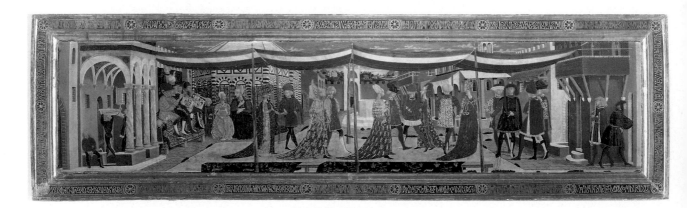

CONVENT AND CHURCH OF SAN MARCO

The **Convent** already existed in the 12th century. In 1437 Cosimo the Elder commissioned Michelozzo with the restructuration and it therefore became the first Florentine convent structure to be built in elegant essential Renaissance form. The lovely **Cloister** has simple elements in stone with brick cornices; on the ground floor the space is enclosed by airy arcades. On the first floor there are fine *lunettes* frescoed by Poccetti, Rosselli, Coccapani, Vanni, Cerrini, Dandini and other illustrious artists. The main entrance to the convent lies to the right of the **Church of San Marco**. This too was restored in 1437 by Michelozzo. It was later renovated by Giambologna (1580) and then by Silvani (1678). The simple facade was redone between 1777 and 1780 by Gioacchino Pronti. The linear interior has an outstanding carved and gilded *ceiling*. Of interest is the **Sacristy**, which contains the sarcophagus with the bronze statue of *St. Antoninus* (1608), and the adjacent **Chapel of St. Antoninus**, decorated by Giambologna, Francavilla, Alessandro

Allori; the frescoes in the dome are by Poccetti. But the true center of attraction of this religious complex is without doubt the Convent. It is well known that an exceptional artist, Fra Angelico, lived and worked within these ancient walls. Most of the frescoes in the **Cloister** (particularly beautiful are the *Crucifix with St. Dominic* at the entrance and the lunette over the door with *St. Peter Martyr*) are his. He also painted the *St. Dominic* in the **Chapter Hall** and a splendid *Crucifixion* inside; a *Pietà* over the door of the **Refectory**; *Jesus as a Pilgrim* over the **Hospice** door, and inside, the *Madonna dell'Arte dei Linaioli*, the *Last Judgement*, the *Stories of Jesus*, the *Deposition*. Through the **Refectory**, with a large fresco by G. A. Sogliani (1536) of the *Crucifixion* and *Providence*, stairs lead to the upper floor, where Fra Angelico's *Annunciation* is most striking. The corridor leads to Michelozzo's **Library** and, at the end of the corridor, to **Cosimo's Cell** with a *Crucifix* by Angelico in the antecell and the *Adoration of the Magi* in the cell. In the corridor to the left is the *Madonna Enthroned with Saints,* and then other splendid works by Fra Angelico are to be found in the cells which open off the corridor; the *Annunciation*, the *Transfiguration, Jesus before the Praetor,* the *Maries at the Sepulcher,* the *Coronation,* the *Presentation in the Temple.* At the end of the corridor is **Savonarola's Cell** (the *Portrait of the martyr* is by Fra Bartolomeo). A staircase to the right leads into the **Small Refectory** with a large fresco of the *Last Supper* by Domenico Ghirlandaio (a version of the more famous one in Ognissanti).

Facing page: the Refectory of S. Marco with the fresco of the Crucifixion and of Providence by Sogliani. Above: Crucifixion by Fra Angelico; below: Last Judgement, also by Fra Angelico.

ARCHAEOLOGICAL MUSEUM

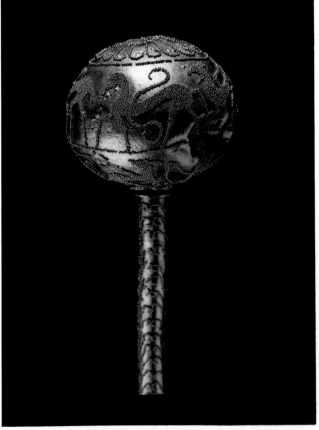

Its rich collections of Egyptian, Etruscan, Greek and Roman art make this museum, which is installed in the 17th-century **Palazzo della Crocetta**, one of Italy's most outstanding. The museum originated with the private collections of the Medicis and of the Grand Dukes. Of particular note in the Egyptian department, which was first instituted in 1824, are the sculpture of the *Goddess Hathor nursing the Pharaoh,* the polychrome relief of the *Goddess Hathor with the Pharaoh Sethos I,* and the bas-relief of the *Goddess of Truth Maat.* Outstanding in the collections of vases and terra cottas in the Graeco-Roman Antiquarium is the famous *François Vase,* a Greek work of the 6th century B.C., found in an Etruscan tomb. The crater, which was probably a wedding gift, was painted by Kleitias and comes from the workshop of the Athenian potter Ergotimos. It was named after Alessandro François who discovered it in Fonte Rutella (Chiusi) in 1845. The vase is decorated with heroic-mythological scenes in black-figure painting. Mention in the Graeco-Roman section must be made of the bronze statue known as *Idolino* (Attic-Peloponnesian school of the 5th cent. B.C.). The collection of Etruscan art, which includes material from more than three hundred years of study, is particularly fine. The collection abounds in sarcophagi, cinerary urns, bronzes, weapons, and objects of daily use. Particularly striking in the field of sculpture are the statue of the *Arringatore,* representing the orator Aulus Metellus,

found near the Trasimene Lake (funerary art of the 3rd century B. C.), and the *Chimaera wounded by Bellerophonte* discovered in Arezzo in 1555, a 5th-century B.C. bronze with the body of a lion and the head of a goat on its back (the tail in the form of a snake is not original).

Facing page, above: the Chimaera of Arezzo; below: an Etruscan pin in gold from Vetulonia. This page, above: the François Vase from Chiusi; below: a gold bracelet from Vetulonia.

On this page (upper left), Palazzo Davanzati with its typical loggia; (right), Palazzo dell'Arte della Lana (headquarters of the wool guild); (lower left), Palazzo Pandolfini on Via San Gallo and (right) Palazzo Cocchi, in Piazza Santa Croce. Opposite (above), Palazzo di Parte Guelfa and Palazzo Antinori; (below), Palazzo Rucellai.

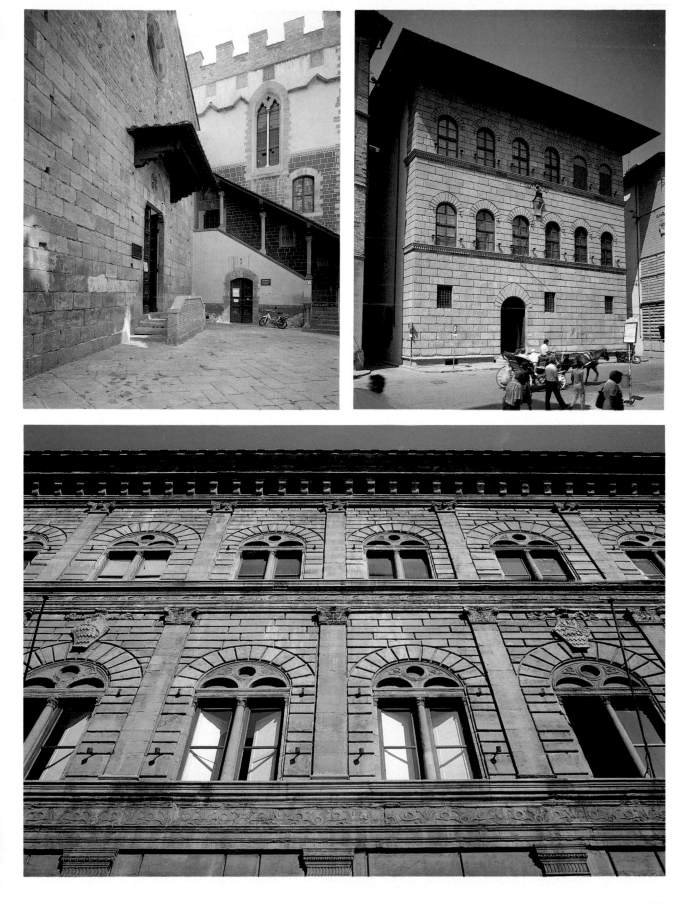

SYNAGOGUE

The Israelite Temple, in an eastern Byzantine style, was designed by the architects Falcini, Treves, Micheli and Cioni (1874). When the large dome was finally covered with copper, it was inaugurated in October of 1882. The construction is interesting both for the elegant frescoes and mosaics which decorate it inside and out, and for its historical and cultural meaning. It is the symbol of the liberation from the ghetto.

PIAZZALE MICHELANGELO

Piazzale Michelangelo is approached from the **Viale dei Colli** that winds its way up the southern slope of Florence for about six kilometers. Both were designed by the architect Giuseppe Poggi in 1868. The Piazzale, a wide terrace overlooking Florence, is centered by a group of bronze figures cast from the original sculptures by Michelangelo (*David* and the four *allegorical statues* that decorate the Medici tombs in the New Sacresty of San Lorenzo).

THE FORTE DI BELVEDERE

Designed by Bernardo Buontalenti (1590-95), the fort was built at the order of Ferdinando I de' Medici on a hilltop dominating Florence for strategic military purposes. It has been restored recently and is used now for important international exhibitions. It offers one of the best views of Florence.

Above: a panoramic view of Florence from Piazzale Michelangelo; left: Forte Belvedere hillside. Opposite: two views of the most important city monuments.

Above: the facade of the Church of S. Miniato al Monte. Left: Michelozzo's Chapel of the Crucifix. Facing page: the interior of the church.

CHURCH OF S. MINIATO AL MONTE

Bishop Hildebrand had the present structure built in 1018 on the site of a 4th-century chapel. The lower part of the facade is decorated by fine arcading; the upper part is simpler and has a fine 12th-century mosaic of *Christ between the Madonna and St. Miniato.* The church, with its unfinished **15th-century campanile** that was damaged during the siege of Florence in 1530, the **Bishop's Palace,** the **fortifications,** the **monumental cemetery** all stand at the top of a hill called Monte alle Croci, which rises up over the Piazzale Michelangelo below and over the entire city. The **interior** of this magnificent example of Florentine Romanesque architecture (it originally belonged to the Benedictine monks and then passed to the Olivetan friars in 1373) is tripartite with a trussed timber roof. Outstanding is the pavement in the center with marble intarsias of *signs of the zodiac* and *symbolic animals.* The walls retain fragments of 13th- and 14th-century *frescoes.* Of note is the **crypt**, a vast space closed off by an elaborate wrought-iron *gate* (1338). The *altar* (11th-cent.) preserves the bones of St. Miniato. Fragments of *frescoes* by Taddeo Gaddi (1341) can be seen in the vaults of the crypt. The raised **presbytery** is of great beauty with its *pulpit* (1207) and an intimate *choir* with fine inlaid wooden choir stalls. The large mosaic of the *Blessing Christ flanked by the Madonna and Saints* (1297) is in the conch of the apse. Entrance to the **Sacristy**, completely

Above: the mosaic with Christ Enthroned in the conch of the apse of S. Miniato. Below: the Crypt. Facing page: two views of the frescoes by Spinello Aretino in the Sacristy.

frescoed by Spinello Aretino (1387) with the sixteen *Stories of the legend of St. Benedict,* is to the right of the presbytery. On the left, stairs lead to the **Chapel of St. James**, or « of the Cardinal of Portugal », designed by Antonio Manetti and decorated with five splendid roundels representing the *Holy Spirit* and the *Cardinal Virtues,* by Luca della Robbia (1461-66). To the right is the *funeral monument of the Cardinal,* a particularly lovely work by Antonio Rossellino (1461). The **Chapel of the Crucifix**, designed by Michelozzo, and with delicate glazed vaulting by Luca della Robbia, stands at the center of the church. To the right of the church is the **Bishop's Palace** (1295-1320), ancient summer residence of the bishops of Florence which then became a convent, a hospital and a Jesuit house.

PALAZZO PITTI

The most imposing of the Florentine palaces dates to 1457 and was probably designed by Brunelleschi. Ammannati enlarged it in the 16th century. The facade (205 m. long and 36 m. high) is covered by a powerful rustication in enormous blocks of stone. The only decorative element are the crowned lion heads set between the window corbels on the ground floor. The two projecting wings date to the period of the Lorrainers. The large arched portal leads through an atrium into Ammannati's **courtyard** which lies lower than the hill of Boboli which with its gardens forms the back of the building. The **Royal apartments** and the **Palatine Gallery** are on the first floor; on the second is the **Gallery of Modern Art**. The palace also contains the **Museo degli Argenti** and the **Museo delle Carrozze**.

BOBOLI GARDENS

These gardens comprise the largest monumental green area in Florence. Their history goes back over four centuries, for Cosimo I commissioned the designs from Niccolo Pericoli, known as Tribolo, in 1549. Work was continued by Ammannati, Buontalenti and Parigi the Younger. Noteworthy places are: **Buontalenti's Grotto** (1583); the **Amphitheater** with the *Roman basin* and the *Egyptian obelisk* at the center; **Neptune's Fishpond**; the statue of *Plenty* by Giambologna and Tacca (1563); the **Grand Duke's Casino**, the **Cavalier's Garden**; Parigi's **Fountain of the Ocean**.

This page: Palazzo Pitti and the piazza. Facing page, above: the Bacchus Fountain and Neptune's Fishpond in the Boboli Gardens; below: the back of Palazzo Pitti.

Facing page, above: the Room of Saturn and, below, the Room of the Niches in Palazzo Pitti. Above: Raphael's Madonna of the Chair in the Palatine Gallery.

PALATINE GALLERY

The Palatine Gallery, which is the second museum for extension and importance after the Uffizi, contains works of enormous value for the history of art. It was realized by Ferdinando II de' Medici with decoration by Pietro da Cortona. The works are placed according to a sixteenth century conception; the pictures are in fact displayed on the walls in an essentially decorative way. The collection was enriched by Cardinal Lorenzo de' Medici, by the last members of the Medici family, and by the Lorrainers. The Gallery is formed of many rooms dedicated to gods and mythological characters depicted in the decorations.

Above, left: Raphael's Madonna del Granduca; right: Madonna and four Saints by Andrea del Sarto. Left: Raphael's Madonna dell'Impannata (of the Linen Window).

Raphael's Donna Velata.

Facing page, above, left: La Gravida, and, right, the Portrait of Maddalena Doni, both by Raphael; below: Madonna and Child by Filippo Lippi.

Right: Four Philosophers, and, below, the Consequences of War, both by Rubens.

Above, left: Vision of Ezekiel by Raphael; right: Assumption with Apostles and Saints by Andrea del Sarto. Left: Holy Family by Andrea del Sarto. Facing page: the two pictures with the Stories of Joseph hebrew by Andrea del Sarto.

CENACOLO OF GHIRLANDAIO

One of Ghirlandaio's masterpieces is to be seen in the **Refectory** of the **Church of Ognissanti** (built in 1256 but thoroughly remodelled in the 17th cent.), after passing through Michelozzo's **Cloister**. This painting of the *Last Supper* (1480) is characterized by the new approach in describing the poses of the Apostles and the use of a landscape (delicate and serene) behind them. These elements may have influenced Leonardo da Vinci who saw the painting two years before leaving Florence.

CHURCH OF CESTELLO

The Church of S. Frediano in Cestello, even though the facade was never finished, is a rare example of the Baroque in Florence. It was built by Antonio Maria Ferri (on a design by the Roman Cerutti), 1680-89. The cupola on a drum (1698) is also his. Inside, the fine fresco in the cupola is by Gabbiani (1701-1718). The church is probably called Cestello because of the vicinity of Cosimo III's Granary, which stands on the eastern side of the square.

CHURCH OF S. SPIRITO

S. Spirito was meant by Brunelleschi to be a twin to S. Lorenzo, but the facade was never finished. The **dome** too is by Brunelleschi while the **campanile** is by Baccio d'Agnolo (1503). The interior is one of the finest examples of Renaissance architecture.

Left: the Church of Ognissanti. Below: Ghirlandaio's Last Supper in the Refectory adjacent to the church. Facing page, above: the Church of S. Frediano in Cestello, and, below, the Church of S. Spirito.

INDEX

History .... page 3

CHURCHES:

Cathedral .... » 5
— Facade .... » 6
— Interior .... » 8
— Dome .... » 5
— Santa Reparata .... » 10
Church of Cestello .... » 120
Church of Orsanmichele .... » 73
Church of S. Croce .... » 45
Church of S. Lorenzo .... » 78
Church of S. Marco .... » 95
Church of S. Maria Novella .... » 74
— Interior .... » 74
— Spanish Chapel .... » 77
Church of S. Miniato al Monte ..... » 106
Church of S. Spirito .... » 120
Church of S. Trinita .... » 124
Church of the Carmine .... » 122
— Brancacci Chapel: the restoration .... » 122
Church of the SS. Annunziata ...... » 89
Pazzi Chapel .... » 52
Other Churches .... » 125
FIESOLE .... » 127

GALLERIES AND MUSEUMS:

Archaeological Museum .... » 98
Galleria degli Uffizi .... » 54
Galleria dell'Accademia .... » 90
Museo dell'Opera del Duomo .... » 22
Museo di S. Croce .... » 52
Museo Nazionale del Bargello ...... » 39
Palatine Gallery .... » 113

MONUMENTS:

Baptistery .... » 13
— Gates of Paradise .... » 14
— Interior .... » 19
Boboli Gardens .... » 110
Bridge and Square of Santa Trinita .... » 71
Bridges of Florence and the Ponte Vecchio .. » 66
Cenacolo of Ghirlandaio .... » 120
Convent of S. Marco .... » 95
Giotto's Campanile .... » 6
Medici Chapels .... » 80
Piazza della Repubblica .... » 71
Piazza della Signoria .... » 26
— Loggia dei Lanzi .... » 29
— Perseus .... » 29
— Cosimo I de' Medici .... » 30
Piazzale Michelangelo .... » 102
Piazza SS. Annunziata .... » 88
Synagogue .... » 102
The Forte di Belvedere .... » 102
The Mannelli Tower .... » 68

PALACES:

Palazzo del Bargello .... » 39
Palazzo Medici-Riccardi .... » 87
Palazzo Pitti .... » 110
Palazzo Strozzi .... » 71
Palazzo Vecchio .... » 30
— Facade .... » 3.
— Interior .... » 3
— Salone dei Cinquecento .... »
— Sala dei Gigli .... »
— Judith: a restored work of art .... »

CHURCH OF THE CARMINE

The 14th-century church of S. Maria del Carmine was almost completely destroyed in a fire in 1771. The **Brancacci Chapel** in the right transept contains a fresco cycle painted between 1425 and 1428 by Masolino and, above all, by Masaccio (the *Temptation* is by the former; the famous *Expulsion from Paradise* and a series of scenes from the *Life of St. Peter,* including the well-known *Tribute Money,* are by the latter). The frescoes were finished by Filippino Lippi.

BRANCACCI CHAPEL: THE RESTORATION

The chapel preserves the most exalting cycle of frescoes known to western art, thanks to the presence of as extraordinary a painter as Masaccio who worked there from 1425 to 1427, in collaboration with Masolino, and the fact that it was finished more than 50 years later by Filippino Lippi. Recent restoration has eliminated retouching and over-painting of the past which had turned the colors into a heavy monochrome, and has restored the frescoes to what they originally were, where form, color and brilliance are marvellously balanced, as is evident in these two details taken from Masaccio's Tribute Money and Masolino's Resurrection of Tabitha.

Left: the facade of the Church of the Carmine. Below, left: the nave of the Church, and, right, the frescoed dome.

Facing page: views of the frescoes in the Brancacci Chapel, once more to be seen in their original splendor thanks to recent meticulous restoration.

Above: the facade of the Church of S. Trinita. Left: the Adoration of the Shepherds by Ghirlandaio.

CHURCH OF S. TRINITA

The 11th-century building was rebuilt and enlarged in the 13th and 14th centuries. The linear facade in stone is by Buontalenti (1593). Thanks to the fact that it stands between the Via Tornabuoni and the Ponte S. Trinita, it is one of the best known churches in Florence. Tradition ascribes the project to Andrea Pisano, the result of the remodelling of a Vallombrosan convent that already stood on the site. The simple lean interior houses important works of art such as the *Madonna and Saints* by Neri di Bicci (1491), the *Annunciation* by Lorenzo Monaco (1425), and Ghirlandaio's *Adoration of the Shepherds* (1485). The frescoes in the **Sassetti Chapel** (1483-1486) are also by Ghirlandaio. The *tombs* of the Sassetti family are by Giuliano da Sangallo. The second chapel to the left of the high altar (with a *triptych* by Mariotto di Nardo, 1416) contains the tomb *of the Bishop of Fiesole* by Luca della Robbia (1454-1456).

OTHER CHURCHES

In the pictures, from the top, the **Church of S. Salvatore al Vescovo**, built after 1000, the facade is Romanesque with blind arcades; the **Church of Badia**, built in 978, the portal with a 16th-century lunette is by Benedetto da Rovezzano (1495); and the **Church of S. Carlo dei Lombardi** built between the 14th and 15th century by Benci di Cione, Neri di Fioravante and Simone Talenti. At the bottom, the **Church of S. Salvi**, built as an abbey in 1048, remodeled many times; the **Church of SS. Apostoli**, built in the 11th century with a Romanesque facade, remarkable the interior; and the **Church of S. Gaetano**, whose elevation is the result of the 17th-century restoration by Gherardo Silvani.

Facing page, above: view of the two knolls of Fiesole; below:
Piazza Mino da Fiesole. This page, above: the Church of
S. Francesco, and, right, the Roman Theater.

...t Etruscan city, standing on its hill, dominates
...he center consists of the beautiful **Piazza Mino**
...where the **Cathedral of S. Romolo** is situated.
... founded in the 11th century, contains the
...el, with frescoes of the 15th century by
...lli and the tomb of Bishop Salutati, by Mino
...e **Bishop's Palace** (11th cent.) and the old
...Maria Primerana** lie across from the
...far off is the **Church** and the **Convent of S.**
... cent.), which houses the **Ethnographic**
...sions** with important Etruscan finds. The
... **Civic Museum** and the wonderful **Roman**
...to the 1st century B.C., can be rapidly
...he square. Nowadays the theater is usually
...ous theatrical and cinematographical
...are the **Roman Baths** and the **Etrusco-**
... The **Bandini Museum** with its sculptures
...om the 13th to the 15th century and the
...**lessandro** must not be overlooked.

127